EASIEST KEYBOARD COLLECTION

Paul Simon

AMSCO PUBLICATIONS
part of The Music Sales Group
London/New York/Paris/Sydney/Copenhagen/Berlin/Madrid/Tokyo

Published by
Amsco Publications

Exclusive Distributors:
Music Sales Corporation
257 Park Avenue South,
New York, NY 10010 USA.
Music Sales Limited
14-15 Berners Street,
London W1T 3LJ, UK.
Music Sales Pty Limited
120 Rothschild Avenue,
Rosebery, NSW 2018,
Australia.

Order No. PS11616
ISBN 13: 978-1-84772-030-6
This book © Copyright 2007 Amsco Publications.

Compiled by Nick Crispin.
Edited by Heather Slater.
Music arranged by Vasco Hexel.
Music processed by Paul Ewers Music Design.

Printed in the United States of America by
Vicks Lithograph and Printing Corporation.

Your Guarantee of Quality
As publishers, we strive to produce every book to the highest
commercial standards.
The music has been freshly engraved and the book has been carefully
designed to minimize awkward page turns and to make playing from
it a real pleasure.
Particular care has been given to specifying acid-free, neutral-sized
paper made from pulps which have not been elemental chlorine
bleached. This pulp is from farmed sustainable forests and was
produced with special regard for the environment.
Throughout, the printing and binding have been planned to ensure
a sturdy, attractive publication which should give years of enjoyment.
If your copy fails to meet our high standards, please inform us and
we will gladly replace it.

www.musicsales.com

Contents

50 WAYS TO LEAVE YOUR LOVER

Words & Music by Paul Simon

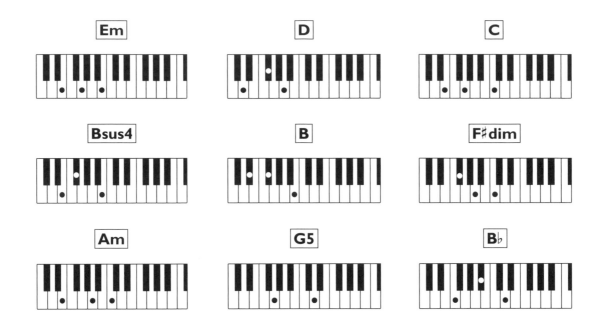

Voice: **Alto Sax**

Rhythm: **Blues Rock**

Tempo: ♩ = 102

"The prob - lem is all in - side___ your head," she said to me.___

The ans - wer is ea - sy if you take it lo - gic - ally.___ I'd like to help___ you in your

strug - gle to___ be free. There must be fif - ty ways___ to leave your lo - ver.___

She said, "It's real-ly not__ my ha-bit to__ in-trude.__ Fur-ther-more,__

__ I hope my mean-ing won't_ be lost__ or mis-cons-trued." But I'll re-peat my-self at the

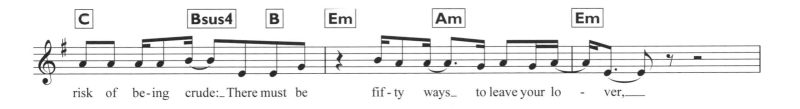

risk of be-ing crude:_ There must be fif-ty ways_ to leave your lo - ver,__

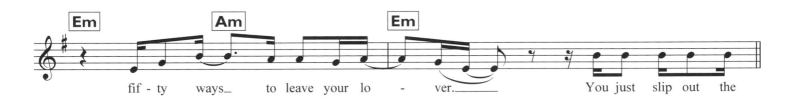

fif-ty ways_ to leave your lo - ver.____ You just slip out the

back, Jack. Make a new plan, Stan. You don't need to be coy,__ Roy. Just lis-ten to

me. Hop on the bus, Gus, you don't need to dis-cuss__ much.____ Just drop off the

key,__ Lee, and get your-self free.

1. slip out the

2. free.

THE 59TH STREET BRIDGE SONG (FEELIN' GROOVY)

Words & Music by Paul Simon

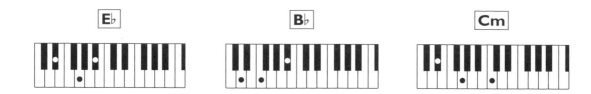

Voice: **Piano**

Rhythm: **Shuffle**

Tempo: ♩ = 146

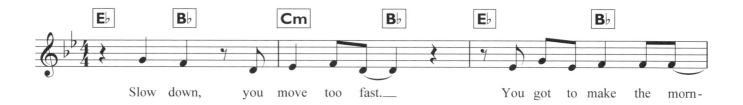

Slow down, you move too fast.___ You got to make the morn-

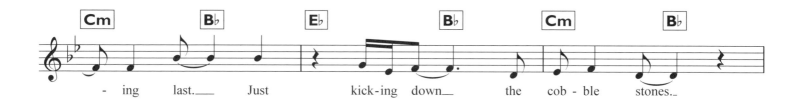

-ing last.___ Just kick-ing down___ the cob-ble stones.___

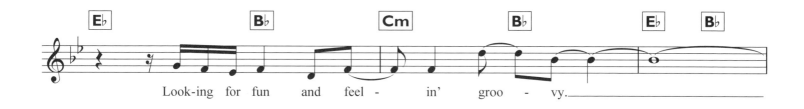

Look-ing for fun and feel-in' groo-vy._____

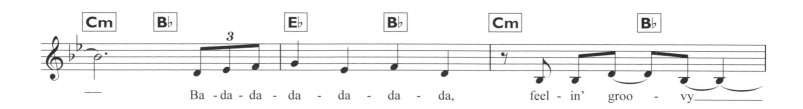

___ Ba-da-da-da-da-da-da, feel-in' groo-vy___

Hel-lo lamp-post,___

what cha know - ing?___ I've come to watch your flow – ers grow – ing.___

Ain't cha got no___ rhymes for me? Doot-in' doo-doo - doo, feel -

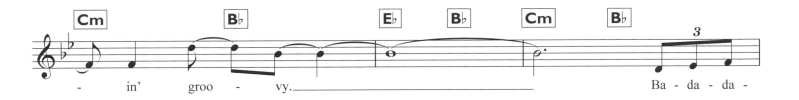

- in' groo - vy.___ Ba - da - da -

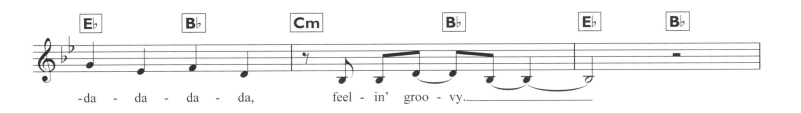

-da - da - da - da - da, feel - in' groo - vy.___

I got no deeds to do, No pro - mi - ses to keep. I'm

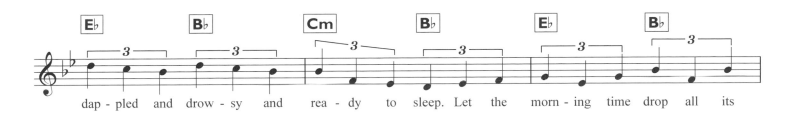

dap - pled and drow - sy and rea - dy to sleep. Let the morn - ing time drop all its

pe - tals on me. Life,___ I love you,___ all is groo - vy.___

AMERICA

Words & Music by Paul Simon

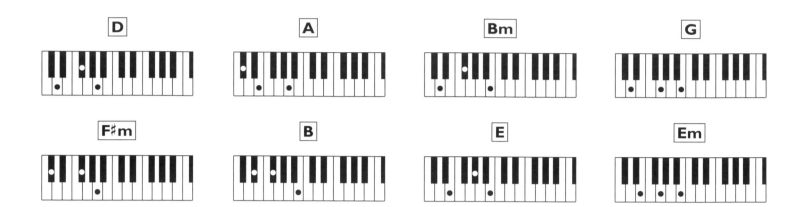

Voice: **Acoustic Guitar**

Rhythm: **Waltz**

Tempo: ♩ = 170

Let us___ be lov - ers:___ we'll mar - ry our for - tunes to - ge - ther.

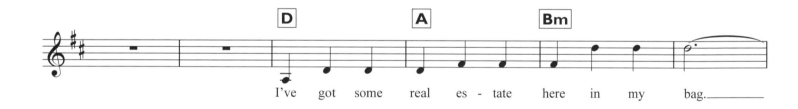

I've got some real es - tate here in my bag.___

So we bought a pack of ci - ga - rettes and

Mis - ses Wag - ner pies___ and walked off to

look for A - me - - ri - ca.

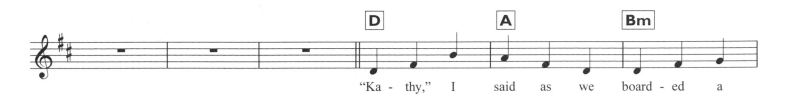

"Ka - thy," I said as we board - ed a

Grey - hound in Pitts - burgh, "Mi - chi - gan

seems like a dream to me now." It took me

four days to hitch - hike from Sa - gi - naw. I've gone to look for A -

Instrumental

- me - - ri - ca.

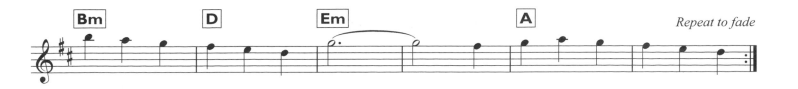

Repeat to fade

THE BOXER

Words & Music by Paul Simon

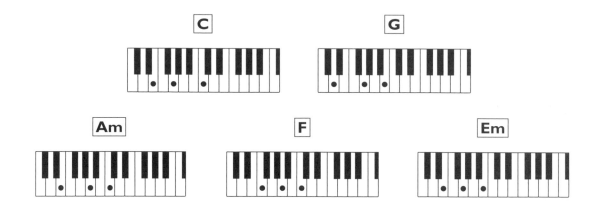

Voice: **Harmonica**

Rhythm: **Country Rock**

Tempo: ♩ = 94

I am just___ a poor___ boy though my sto-ry's sel-dom told. I have

squan-dered my re-sis-tance___ for a pock-et-ful of mumb-les, such are

pro-mi-ses. All lies and jest, still the man___ hears___ what he

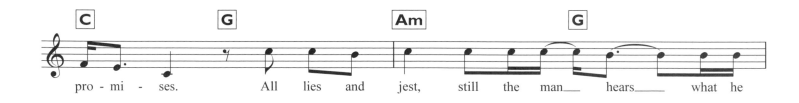

wants to hear___ and dis-re-gards___ the rest, hmm...___

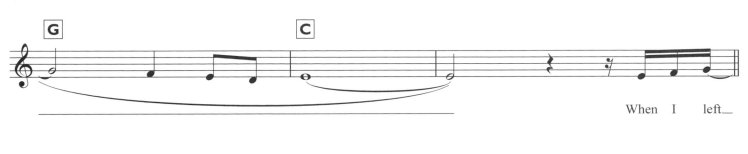

When I left___

___ my home___ and my fa - mi - ly,____ I was no more than a boy in the

com - pa - ny of stran - gers,____ in the qui - et of the rail - way sta - tion,

run - ning scared.___ Lay - ing low, seek - ing out___

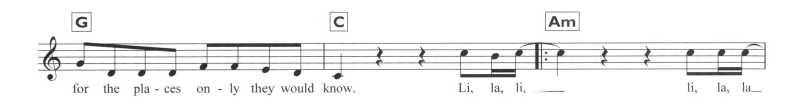

___ the poor - er quar - ters, where the rag - ged peo - ple go, look - ing

for the pla - ces on - ly they would know. Li, la, li,___ li, la, la___

Em   Am   G   *Repeat to fade*

___ la, li la, li,___ li, la, li,___ li, la, la,___ la, li, la, li,___ la, la, la, la, li,___

BRIDGE OVER TROUBLED WATER

Words & Music by Paul Simon

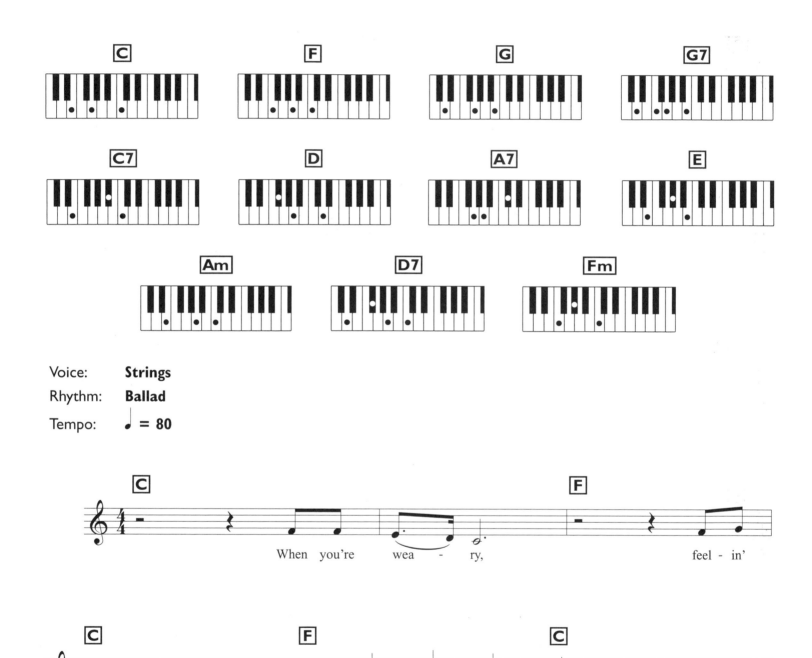

Voice: **Strings**

Rhythm: **Ballad**

Tempo: ♩ = **80**

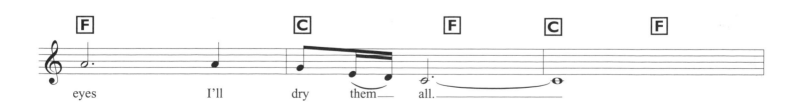

CECILIA

Words & Music by Paul Simon

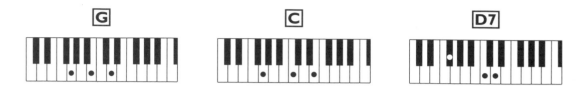

Voice: **Banjo**

Rhythm: **Rock**

Tempo: ♩ = 108

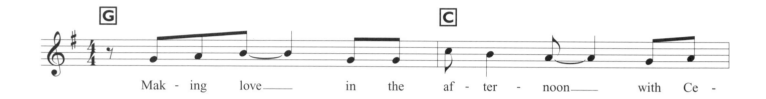

Mak - ing love ___ in the af - ter - noon ___ with Ce -

- ci - lia up ___ in my bed - room. ___ I got up ___ to

wash my face ___ when I come back to bed ___ some-one's tak - en my place. ___

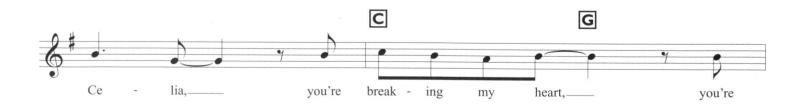

Ce - lia, ___ you're break - ing my heart, ___ you're

shak - ing my con - fi - dence dai - ly. ___ Oh Ce -

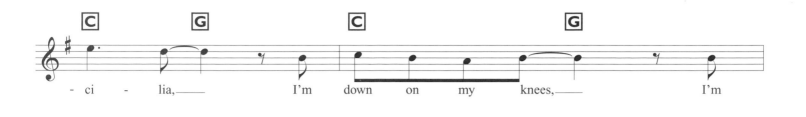

- ci - lia,_____ I'm down on my knees,_____ I'm

beg - ging you please_____ to come home,_____ come on home._____ Poh poh

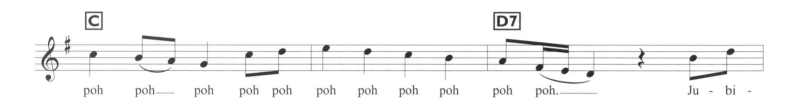

poh poh_____ poh poh poh poh poh poh poh poh._____ Ju - bi -

- la - tion,_____ she loves me a - gain,_____ I fall on the floor_____ and I'm laugh-

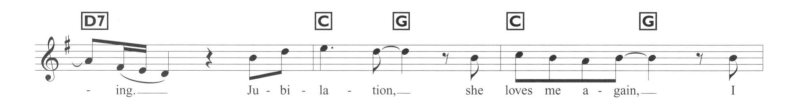

- ing._____ Ju - bi - la - tion,_____ she loves me a - gain,_____ I

fall on the floor_____ and I'm laugh - ing._____ Oh oh oh oh,_____ oh

oh oh oh oh,_____ oh oh oh oh oh_____ oh oh oh. Oh oh

DIAMONDS ON THE SOLES OF HER SHOES

Words & Music by Paul Simon
© Copyright 1986 Paul Simon. All Rights Reserved. International Copyright Secured.

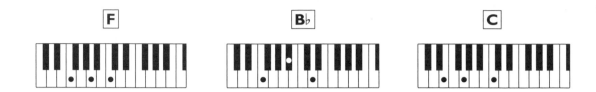

Voice: **Alto Sax**

Rhythm: **Disco Pop**

Tempo: ♩ = 114

Peo-ple say she's cra - zy: She got dia - monds on the soles of her shoes.

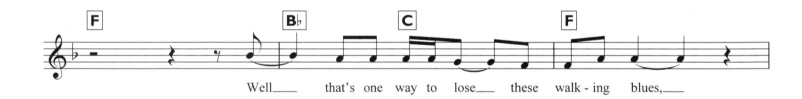

Well___ that's one way to lose___ these walk - ing blues,___

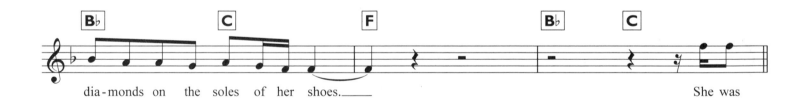

dia-monds on the soles of her shoes.___ She was

phy - si - cally___ for - got - ten,___ and then she slipped in - to my pock - et with my car

keys.___ She said "you've tak - en me for grant - ed be - cause

I please_____ you_____ wear - ing these dia - - - -

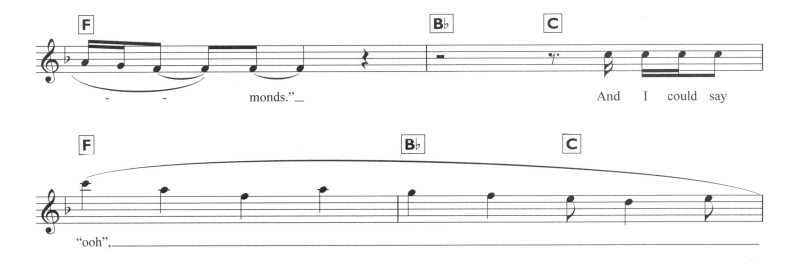

- - - monds."__

And I could say

"ooh",_____

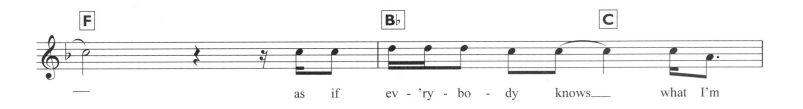

— as if ev - 'ry - bo - dy knows____ what I'm

talk - ing__ a - bout.____ As if ev - 'ry - bo - dy here would know ex - act - ly what I

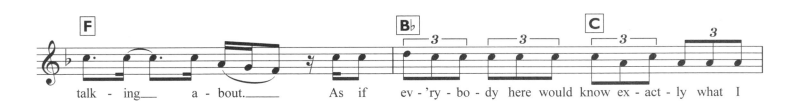

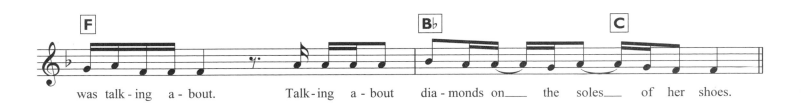

was talk - ing__ a - bout. Talk - ing a - bout dia - monds on____ the soles____ of her shoes.

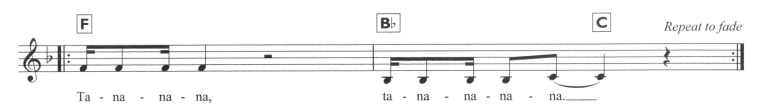

Repeat to fade

Ta - na - na - na,

ta - na - na - na - na.____

A HAZY SHADE OF WINTER

Words & Music by Paul Simon

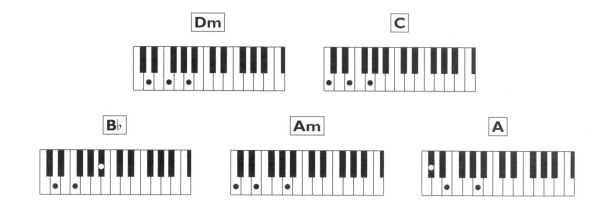

Voice: **Acoustic Guitar**

Rhythm: **Rock**

Tempo: ♩ = 146

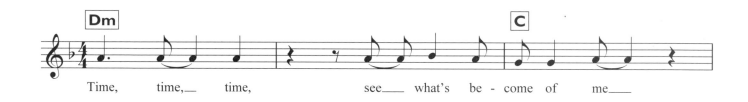

Time, time,— time, see— what's be - come of me—

while I—— looked a - round— for my— pos - si -

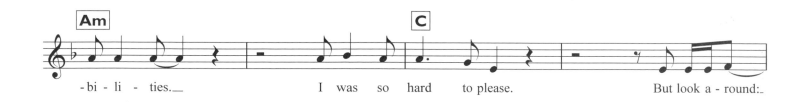

-bi - li - ties.— I was so hard to please. But look a - round:—

— leaves— are brown and the sky— is a ha - zy shade— of win-

-ter.__ Hear_ the Sal - va - tion Ar - my__ band_

down by the ri - ver - side.__ It's bound to be a bet - ter ride_ than what you've_ got planned.

Car - ry___ your cup in___ your hand and look a - round_

__ you:_ leaves are brown_ now_ and the sky___ is a ha - zy shade_ of win -

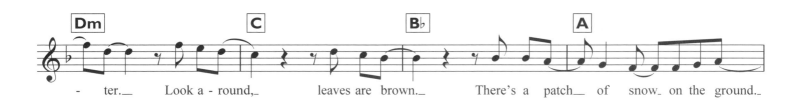

- ter.__ Look a - round,__ leaves are brown.__ There's a patch_ of snow_ on the ground.__

__ Look a - round,___ leaves are brown.__ There's a patch_

1.

2.

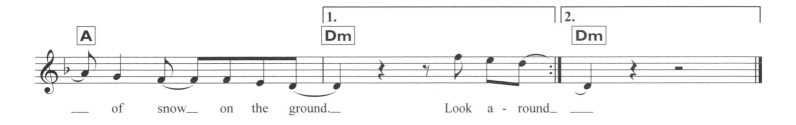

__ of snow_ on the ground.__ Look a - round_ ___

HOMEWARD BOUND

Words & Music by Paul Simon

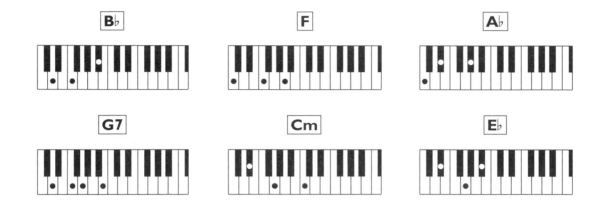

Voice: **Acoustic Guitar**

Rhythm: **Skiffle**

Tempo: ♩ = 90

I'm sit-ting in__ the rail-way sta-ion. Got a tick-et for__ my des - ti - na - tion,__

__ mhm...,__ on a tour__ of one - night stands, my

suit-case and gui-tar__ in hand,__ and ev-'ry stop__ is neat - ly planned for a po-et and__ a one - man band.__

__ Home - ward bound,__ I wish I__ was,__ home - ward

I AM A ROCK

Words & Music by Paul Simon

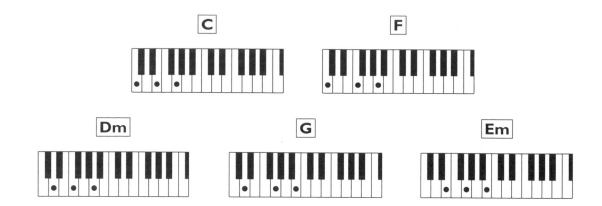

Voice: **Rock Organ**

Rhythm: **Hard Rock**

Tempo: ♩ = 118

A win-ter's day   in a

deep and dark   De-cem-ber.

I am a-lone,   gaz-ing from my win-dow

to the streets be-low on a fresh-ly fall-en sil-ent shroud of snow. I am a rock,

I am an is - - - - land.

I've built walls,_____ a

fort - ress deep__ and migh - ty,__ that

none_____ may_____ pe - ne - trate. I have no need of friend - ship,__

friend-ship cau - ses pain. It's laugh-ter and it's lov-ing I dis - dain. I am a rock,_

I am an is - - - - land.

And a rock feels_ no pain. And an is - land__ ne - ver cries.

KATHY'S SONG

Words & Music by Paul Simon

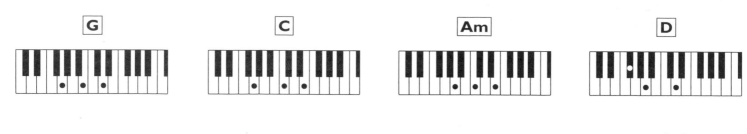

Voice: **Flute**

Rhythm: **Rock 2**

Tempo: ♩ = 100

I hear the driz - zle of the rain:___ like a

me - mo - ry it falls.___ Soft and warm con - ti - nu - ing,___

___ tap - ping on my___ roof and walls.___

And from the shel - ter of my mind,___ through the

win - dow___ of my eyes,___ I gaze be - yond the

rain-drenched streets___ to Eng - land___ where my heart lies.___

My mind's dis - trac - ted and___ dif - fused.___ My thoughts are

ma - ny miles a - way.___ They lie with you when

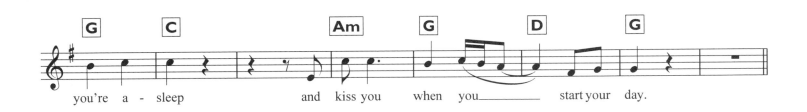

you're a - sleep and kiss you when you___ start your day.

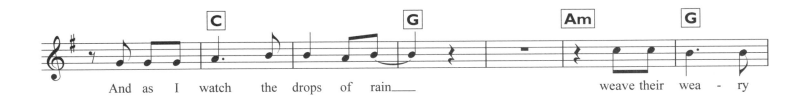

And as I watch the drops of rain___ weave their wea - ry

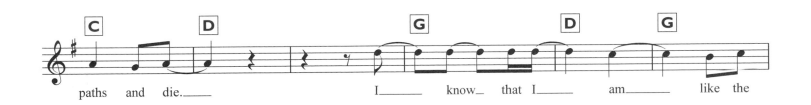

paths and die.___ I___ know___ that I___ am___ like the

rain: there but for the grace___ of you___ go I.___

KODACHROME™

Words & Music by Paul Simon

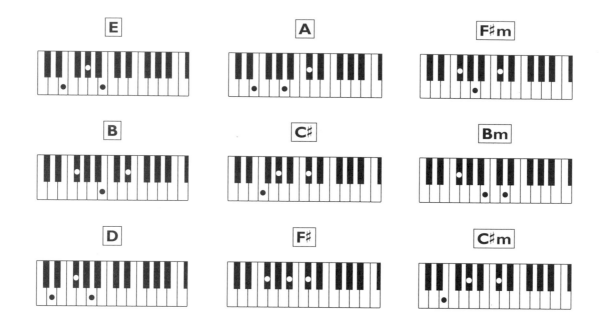

Voice: **Honky-Tonk Piano**

Rhythm: **House**

Tempo: ♩ = 140

When I think back on all the crap I learned in high school

it's a won-der I can think at all.

And my lack of e-du-ca-tion has-n't hurt me none:

I can read the writ-ing on the wall. Ko-da-

LOVES ME LIKE A ROCK

Words & Music by Paul Simon

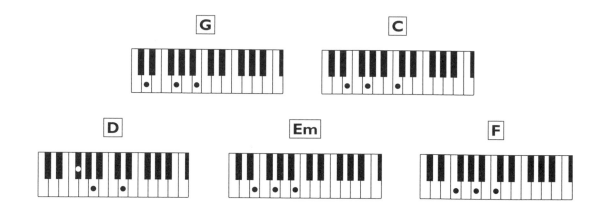

Voice: **Tenor Sax**

Rhythm: **Swing Rock**

Tempo: ♩ = 140

When I was a lit - tle boy, and the de - vil would call my

name I'd say "Now_____

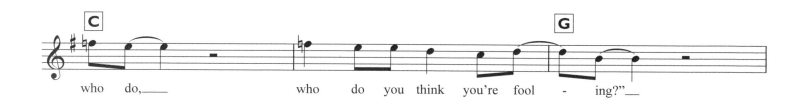

who do,_____ who do you think you're fool - ing?"___

I'm a con - se - cra - ted boy.

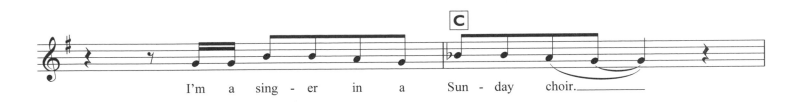

I'm a sing-er in a Sun-day choir._____

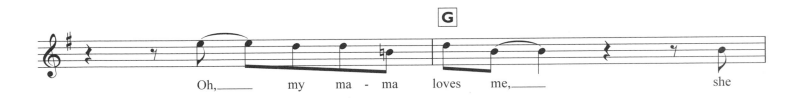

Oh,_____ my ma-ma loves me,_____ she

loves me._____ She get down on her knees and hug_____

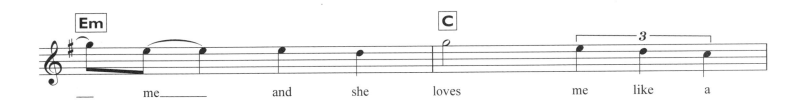

__ me_____ and she loves me like a

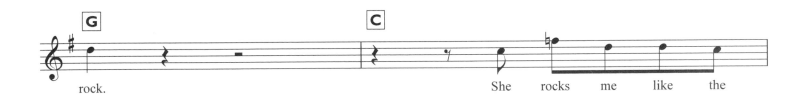

rock. She rocks me like the

rock of a-ges and loves me._____

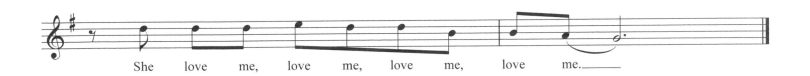

She love me, love me, love me, love me._____

ME AND JULIO DOWN BY THE SCHOOLYARD

Words & Music by Paul Simon

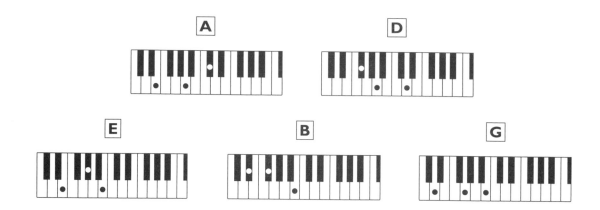

Voice: **Acoustic Guitar**

Rhythm: **Funk**

Tempo: ♩ = 100

The ma-ma pa-ja-ma rolled__ out of bed and she ran to the po-lice sta-tion.

When the pa-pa found out, he be-gan to shout__ and he start-ed the in-ves-ti-ga-

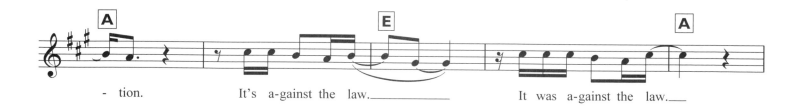

-tion.   It's a-gainst the law._____   It was a-gainst the law.__

What the ma-ma saw,___   it was a-gainst the law.__

Ma - ma looked down and spit on the ground ev -'ry time my name_ gets men - tioned.

The pa - pa said "oi, if I get that boy_ I'm gon - na

stick him in the house of de - ten - tion." Well, I'm on my

way. I don't know where I'm go - ing.____ I'm on my

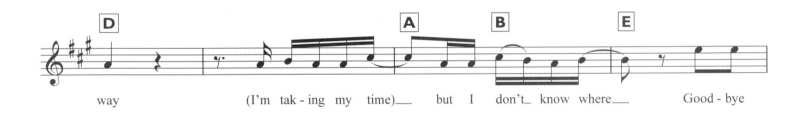

way (I'm tak - ing my time)_ but I don't_ know where____ Good - bye

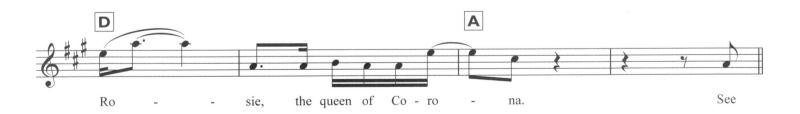

Ro - - sie, the queen of Co - ro - na. See

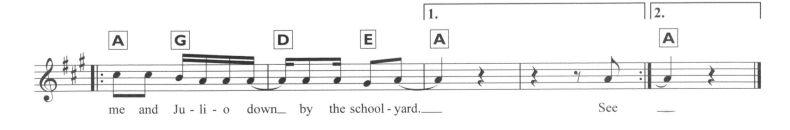

me and Ju - li - o down_ by the school - yard.____ See _

MOTHER AND CHILD REUNION

Words & Music by Paul Simon

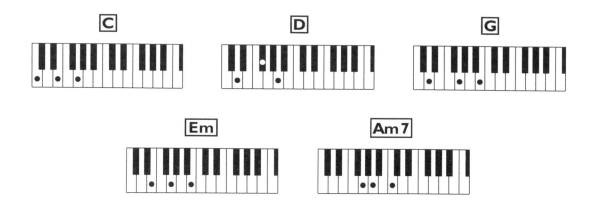

Voice: **Rock Organ**

Rhythm: **Funk**

Tempo: ♩ = 120

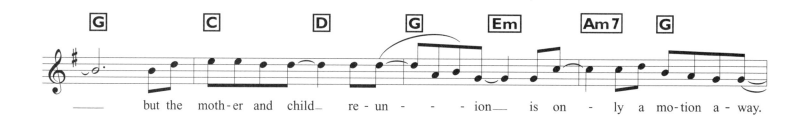

No, I would not give— you false— hope on this strange and mourn-ful day,—

— but the moth-er and child— re-un - - -ion— is on - ly a mo-tion a - way.

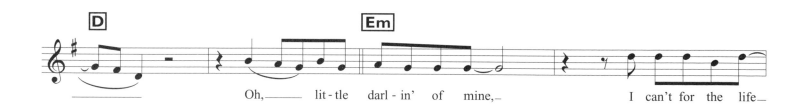

Oh,— lit-tle darl-in' of mine,— I can't for the life—

— of me— re-mem-ber a sad-der day.— I know they say

let it be,_____ but it just don't work out that way, and the course of a

life - time runs_____ ov - er and ov - er a - gain._____ No, I

would not give_____ you false_____ hope on this strange and mourn - ful day,_____ but the

moth-er and child_____ re - un - - ion_____ is on - - ly a mo-tion a - way._____

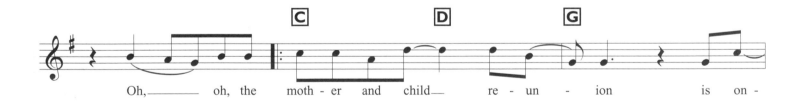

Oh,_____ oh, the moth - er and child_____ re - un - ion is on -

- ly a mo-tion a - way._____ Oh, the moth - er and child_____ re - un -

Repeat to fade

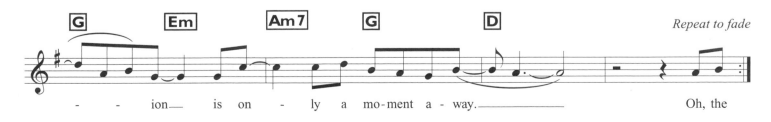

- - ion_____ is on - - ly a mo-ment a - way._____ Oh, the

MRS. ROBINSON

Words & Music by Paul Simon

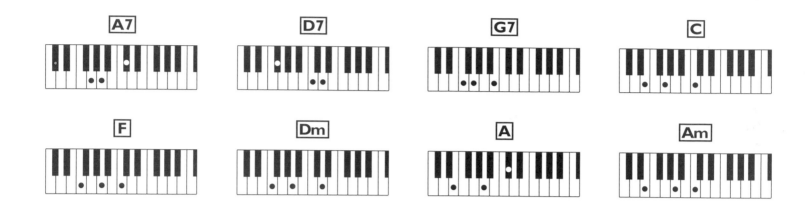

Voice:	**Acoustic Guitar**
Rhythm:	**Rock**
Tempo:	♩ = 104

A7

We'd like to know a lit - tle bit___ a - bout___

D7

___ you for our files.___ We'd like to help you

G7

learn to help your - self.___ Look a - round you, all___

C   F   Dm

___ you see___ are sym - pa - the - tic eyes.___

Stroll a - round the grounds un - til you feel at home.

___ And here's to you___ Mrs___ Rob - in - son,___

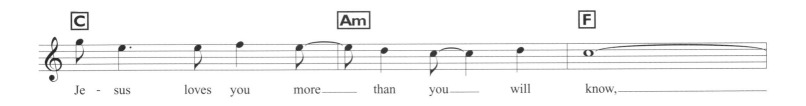

Je - sus loves you more___ than you___ will know,___

___ (wo wo wo.___) God bless you

please Mrs___ Rob - in - son,___ hea - ven holds___ a place___

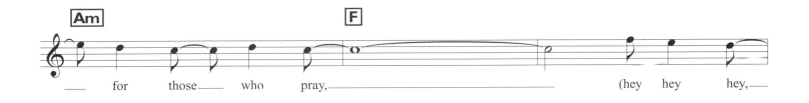

___ for those___ who pray,___ (hey hey hey,___

___ hey hey hey.___)

SCARBOROUGH FAIR/CANTICLE

Traditional
Arrangement & original countermelody by Paul Simon & Art Garfunkel

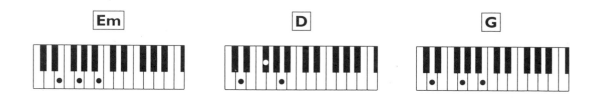

Voice: **Vocal Oohs**

Rhythm: **Waltz**

Tempo: ♩ = 130

Are you go-ing___ to Scar-bo-rough Fair?

(pars-ley, sage, rose-ma-ry and thyme,)___

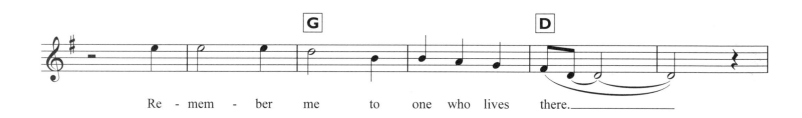

Re-mem-ber me to one who lives there.___

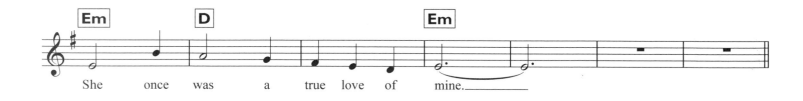

She once was a true love of mine.___

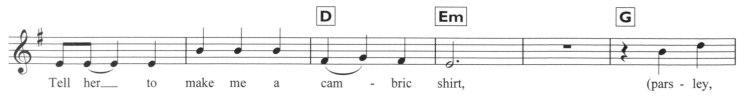

Tell her___ to make me a cam-bric shirt, (pars-ley,

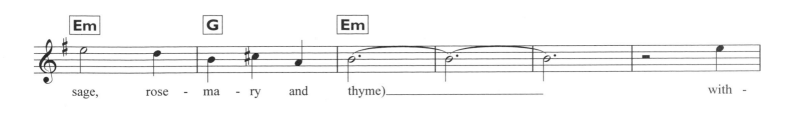

sage, rose - ma - ry and thyme)_____ with -

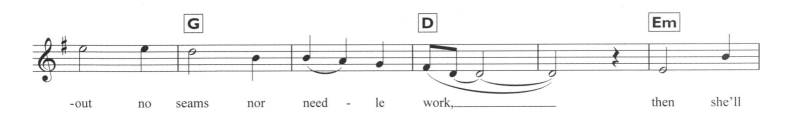

-out no seams nor need - le work,_____ then she'll

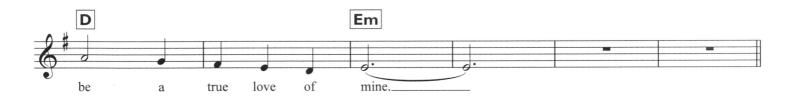

be a true love of mine._____

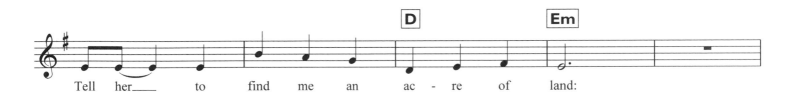

Tell her____ to find me an ac - re of land:

(pars - ley, sage, rose - ma - ry and thyme)_____

be - tween the salt wa - ter and the sea strand,_____

____ then she'll be a true love of mine._____

SLIP SLIDIN' AWAY

Words & Music by Paul Simon
© Copyright 1977 Paul Simon. All Rights Reserved. International Copyright Secured.

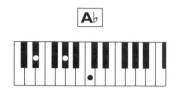
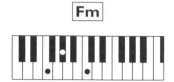
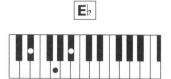
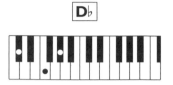

Voice: **Vocal Oohs**

Rhythm: **Pop Ballad**

Tempo: ♩. = 120

Slip slid - in' a - way, slip slid - in' a -

- way._____ You know, the

near - er your des - ti - na - tion, the more___ you slip slid - in' a -

- way. I know a man,___

___ he came from my home - town.

He wore his pas - sion for his wo - man like a thorn - y crown.___

He said "Do - lo - res,_____ I live in

fear._____ My love for you is so ov - er - po - wer - ing, I'm a - fraid_

___ that I_____ will dis - ap - pear." Slip slid - in' a -

- way, slip slid - in' a -

- way._____ You know, the

near - er your des - ti - na - tion, the more___ you slip slid - in' a - way.

SOMETHING SO RIGHT

Words & Music by Paul Simon

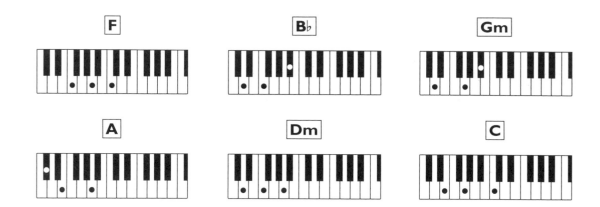

Voice: **Flute**

Rhythm: **Pop**

Tempo: ♩ = 78

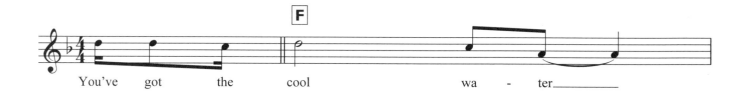

You've got the cool wa - ter

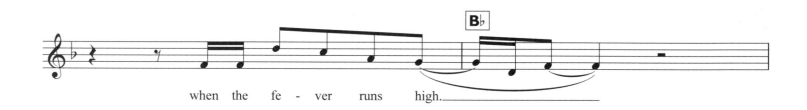

when the fe - ver runs high.

You've got the look of love - light in your eyes.____ And I was in

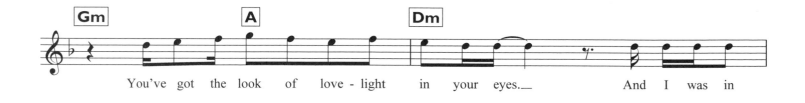

cra - zy mo - tion 'till you calmed me down.____

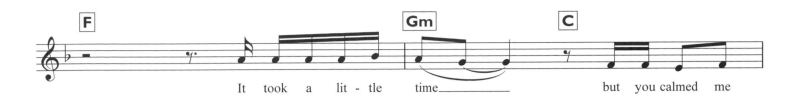

It took a lit - tle time_____ but you calmed me

down. When some - thing goes wrong I'm_____

___ the first to ad - mit it. I'm the first to ad - mit it____

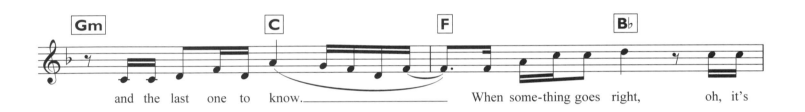

and the last one to know._____ When some-thing goes right, oh, it's

like - ly to lose me,____ mhm.___ It's apt to con - fuse__ me. It's

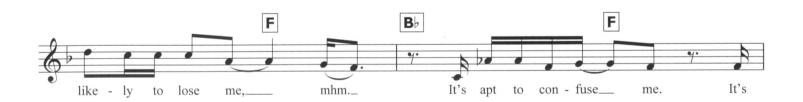

such an un - u - su - al sight. Oh,_____ I can't, I can't get used to some-thing so right,

some - thing so right.

THE SOUND OF SILENCE

Words & Music by Paul Simon

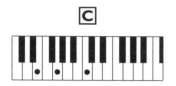
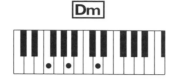
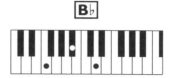
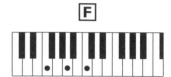

Voice: **Acoustic Guitar**

Rhythm: **Rock**

Tempo: ♩ = 108

Hel - lo dark - ness, my old friend,

I've come to talk with you a - gain.

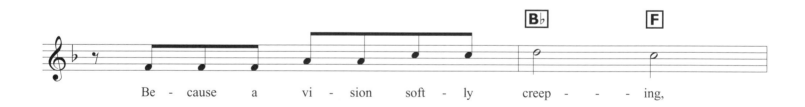

Be - cause a vi - sion soft - ly creep - - ing,

left its seeds while I was sleep - - ing,

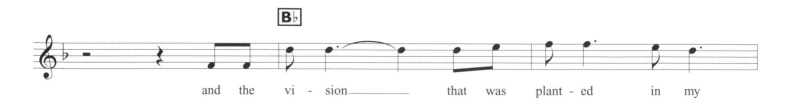

and the vi - sion _____ that was plant - ed in my

STILL CRAZY AFTER ALL THESE YEARS

Words & Music by Paul Simon

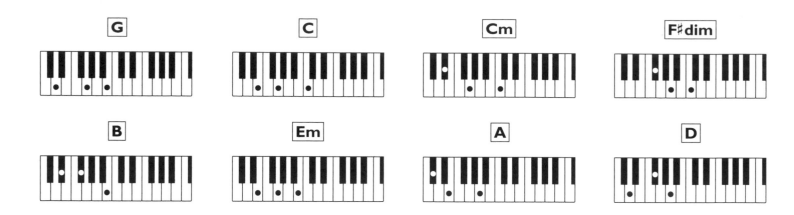

Voice: **Electric Piano**

Rhythm: **Waltz**

Tempo: ♩ = 114

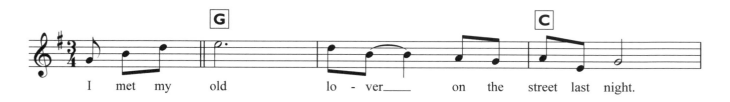

I met my old lo - ver___ on the street last night.

She seemed so glad___ to see me,___ I just smiled.___

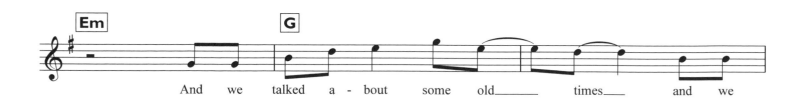

And we talked a - bout some old___ times___ and we

drank our - selves___ some beers. Still cra - zy___ af - ter

all these_____ years. Oh, still

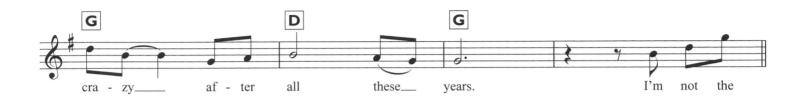

cra - zy_____ af - ter all these__ years. I'm not the

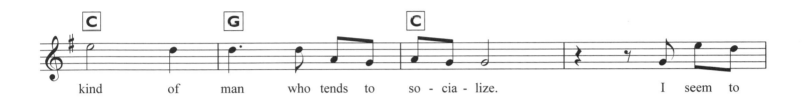

kind of man who tends to so - cia - lize. I seem to

lean on__ old__ fa - mi - liar ways.__ And I

ain't no fool for love songs that whis - per in my

ears. Still cra - zy_____ af - ter all these__ years.

Oh, still cra - zy_____ af - ter all these__ years.

TAKE ME TO THE MARDI GRAS

Words & Music by Paul Simon

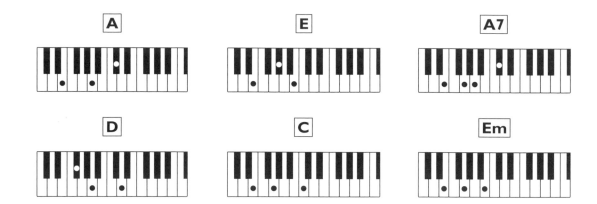

Voice: **Trumpet**

Rhythm: **Dance Pop**

Tempo: ♩ = **100**

Come on take me to the Mar - di Gras___ where the peo - ple sing and

play,_____ where the danc - ing is e - lite___ and there's

mu - sic in the street___ both night and day. Hur - ry, take me to the

Mar - di Gras___ in the ci - ty of my dreams._____ You can

le - ga - lize_ your lows,_ you can wear your sum - mer clothes_ in New Or - leans.

And I will lay my bur - den down,_____ rest my head up - on that shore.

And when I wear that star - ry crown, I won't be want - ing a - ny - more.

Mm... Take your bur - dens to the Mar - di Gras._ Let the mu - sic wash your

soul._____ You can min - gle in_ the street._You can jin - gle to the beat of Jel - ly Roll._

_ Tum - ba, tum - ba, tum - ba, Mar - di Gras_ Tum - ba, tum - ba, tum - ba,

day._____

1 2 3 4 5 6 7 8 9

ENJOY THESE OTHER
PAUL SIMON
SONGBOOKS

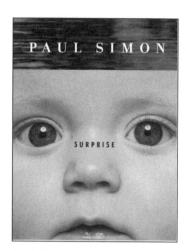

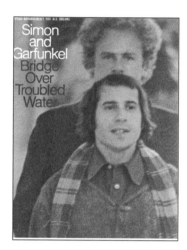

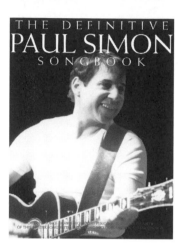

Paul Simon: Surprise
The matching folio to Paul Simon's 2006 album, *Surprise*. Songs include "How Can You Live In The Northeast," "Everything About It Is A Love Song," "Wartime Prayers," "Father And Daughter," and many more. Arranged for piano, vocal and guitar.

ISBN 0.8256.3472.5
ISBN-13: 978.0.8256.3472.7
PS11605

Paul Simon:
Bridge Over Troubled Water
Specially arranged music from the Grammy award winning album, *Bridge Over Troubled Water*. Songs include: "Bridge Over Troubled Water," "Baby Driver," "The Only Living Boy In New York," "Cecilia," and many more.

ISBN 0.7119.0205.4
ISBN-13: 978.0.7119.0205.3
PS10172

The Definitive Paul Simon Songbook
Over 150 songs drawn from every period in the unique career of this master songwriter. Each song includes melody, guitar chords, and complete lyrics. Contains "America," "Bridge Over Troubled Water," "Cecilia," "The Sound Of Silence," and many more favorites!

ISBN 0.8256.3323.0
ISBN-13: 978.0.8256.3323.2
PS11594

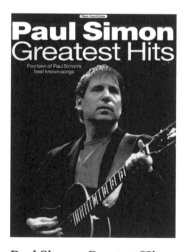

Paul Simon: Anthology
50 favorites arranged for piano/vocal and guitar. Includes: "The Boy In The Bubble," "Bridge Over Troubled Water," "Everything Put Together Falls Apart," "Hearts And Bones," "Loves Me Like A Rock," "The Sound Of Silence," and more.

ISBN 0.8256.1278.0
ISBN-13: 978.0.8256.1278.7
PS11196

Paul Simon: Greatest Hits
This songbook contains 14 of Paul Simon's best songs including "The Boxer," "Crazy Love Vol.II," "El Condor Pasa (If I Could)," "59th Street Bridge Song (Feelin' Groovy)," "Homeward Bound," and more!
Arranged for piano and vocal with guitar boxes.

ISBN 0.7119.7912.X
ISBN-13: 978.0.7119.7912.3
PS11477

Classic Paul Simon:
The Simon And Garfunkel Years
A collection of all the music from four landmark Simon and Garfunkel albums: *The Sound Of Silence*; *Parsley, Sage, Rosemary, And Thyme*; *Bookends*; and *Bridge Over Troubled Water*. Arranged for piano/vocal with guitar frames and lyrics.

ISBN 0.8256.3311.7
ISBN-13: 978.0.8256.3311.9
PS11253

§ *The* **Music Sales** *Group*

TO ORDER: Distribution Center • 445 Bellvale Road • Chester, NY 10918
Tel 800-431-7187 • Fax 800-345-6842 • info@musicsales.com • www.musicsales.com